Frisco Farm Corp. v. Blenheim Markets

Case File

Trial Materials

FRISCO FARM CORP. V. BLENHEIM MARKETS

Case File

Trial Materials

ANTHONY J. BOCCHINO
Jack E. Feinberg Professor of Litigation, Emeritus
Temple University School of Law

DEANNE C. SIEMER
Managing Director, Wilsie Co. LLC
Washington, D.C.

NITA®
NATIONAL INSTITUTE FOR TRIAL ADVOCACY

Address inquiries to:
Reprint Permission
National Institute for Trial Advocacy
1685 38th Street, Suite 200
Boulder, CO 80301-2735
Phone: (800) 225-6482
Fax: (720) 890-7069
Email: permissions@nita.org

ISBN 978-1-60156-938-7
FBA1938
eISBN 978-1-60156-940-0
FBA1940

ASPEN PUBLISHING

Official co-publisher of NITA.
aspenpublishing.com/NITA

ACKNOWLEDGMENTS

The authors acknowledge the learning and practical teaching advice they have accumulated over the years working with colleagues on many NITA, ABA, and law firm trial advocacy programs. Since the early 1970s, NITA's programs and published materials have brought skills training to lawyers in all kinds of trial practices around the country and to students in law school trial advocacy classes. That public service effort has been a unique contribution to the profession.

The authors are extremely grateful to NITA editor Virginia Judd, J.D., and the extraordinary application of insight, intelligence, unequaled editing skills, collegiality and, most important, good humor and patience that she applied to this project. On this and every project on which we have had the opportunity to work with her, the result has been a better, more concise and informative end product.

Dedication

Anthony Bocchino

To Genevieve and Bella—The Next Generation

Deanne Seimer

To Finn, Jackson, and Max

Contents

Introduction

Frisco Farm Corp. is a fresh produce broker operating in the state of Nita. Frisco neither grows agricultural products nor sells them to the public. It is essentially a middleman putting sellers of agricultural products (farmers, co-ops etc.) together with buyers (supermarkets, restaurants, institutions, etc.) who sell to the public. The agricultural brokerage business differs significantly from most brokerages because agricultural brokers typically purchase the product from the agricultural supplier and sell the product (virtually simultaneously) to a pre-identified buyer at a profit.

Frisco's purchasing department identifies available product from farms, co-ops, etc., and communicates that information to the sales department, which has contacts with retail and institutional buyers. The two departments collaborate on a price to offer for the product, based on the producer's asking price, the likely sales point to a buyer, and Frisco's target profit margin. Once all prices (buy/sell) are in place and agreed to internally, Frisco contracts with the producer for the product at the producer's price, contracts with the buyer for Frisco's target price (or better) for delivery of the same product, and arranges for delivery of the product from the producer to the buyer. Frisco's profit on the transaction is the difference of the price to Frisco and the price to Frisco's customer less the cost of shipping. Frisco, like most brokers in this industry, hires independent truckers. The truckers are agents of the broker.

In September of YR-2, Frisco had been in the produce brokering business for over fifteen years. While Frisco employed a few full-time management personnel to oversee its operations, their actual buyers and sellers were a team of about twenty-five part-time employees statewide. Frisco's management team and largest office are located in Nita City.

In September of YR-2, Frisco's buying manager was Madrid Pinto, and the sales manager was Ronnie Gyandoh. Georgie Veramos was one of Frisco's part-time buyers. Addison Rogers, an aspiring actor, was one of Frisco's part-time sellers.

On September 19, YR-2 Veramos learned that the Pomes R Us Farms (PRUF), a very large commercial orchard, had 25,000 pounds of organic Heritage apples that would become available within a week to ten days. Veramos called PRUF and was told the asking price was $4.00 per pound. Veramos notified Pinto, Gyandoh, and Rogers that same day, and on September 20 Rogers contacted Sam Pagano at Blenheim Markets by email. Rogers approached Blenheim, which was not a regular customer of Frisco, because Veramos had said that Blenheim had been having difficulty with its regular supplier and because Blenheim was big enough to take the entire 25,000 pounds available from PRUF.

Rogers told Pagano about the apples. Pagano, without confirming any difficulty with Blenheim's regular supplier, expressed interest in the proposed sale and promised to get back to Rogers within a few days. Rogers confirmed the proposed sale to Pagano in an email. Rogers, at the urging of Gyandoh, hoped to break through with Blenheim, a potential lucrative long-term customer.

Rogers and Veramos agreed that $4.00 per pound was a fair price for Frisco to pay PRUF for organic Heritage apples as they are scarce and highly desirable. They also agreed on an internal target price for selling the apples at $4.60 per pound as that would meet Frisco's target profit margin.

On September 24 Rogers received a phone call from Pagano who agreed to purchase the 25,000 lbs. of Heritage apples at a price of $4.62 per pound, to be delivered to Blenheim's Yard A at 4505 Grocers Way, Conwell, Nita within six days, *unless* Blenheim notified Frisco of cancellation of the agreement within three business days from the confirmation of the agreement via email. Pagano confirmed this in an email to Rogers's Frisco email address on September 24. Rogers confirmed the deal by email to Pagano on the same day.

On September 28, Pagano sent an email to Rogers's email address at Frisco for the purpose of canceling Blenheim's order from Frisco. But Rogers never read Pagano's cancellation because September 25 was Rogers's last day employed at Frisco; Gyandoh did not see the email until September 30. The shipment was sent out September 29.

As broker, Frisco was responsible for delivering the Heritage apples from PRUF to Blenheim. At Pagano's suggestion, Rogers contracted with Farm Fresh Delivery (FFD) for delivery, rather than utilizing one of Frisco's regular trucking services. Rogers chose FFD because Pagano said FFD had the specialized trailer equipment Blenheim liked for transport of agricultural produce like apples, and because FFD was familiar with Blenheim's Conwell yard where the apples were to be delivered.

On September 28, FFD picked up Frisco's apples and brought them to Blenheim's Conwell yard. The apples (by agreement) were to be delivered to Yard A, where orders of apples and other fruit typically were handled. Riley Sturdevant, the delivery driver and child of the owner of FFD, was familiar with the yard and knew fruit deliveries were made to Yard A at the Blenheim Conwell yard.

When FFD arrived at the Blenheim yard in Conwell, Sturdevant showed the gatekeeper the delivery order for Yard A and was allowed in, even though the shipment was not on the gatekeeper's list. The gatekeeper allowed the truck into the facility upon recognizing Sturdevant and the FFD truck and was shown an invoice for the shipment by Sturdevant. Typically, a shipment scheduled for a particular yard at Blenheim was met by a small crew, with scales and a receiving conveyor, who would take delivery from FFD directly from the back of the self-unloading trailer onto the front of the conveyor belt into the storage building. On September 28 however, there was no such crew; Yard A was vacant. Sturdevant searched Frisco's work order form for a contact person at Blenheim, but none was listed. Sturdevant, on a tight schedule for the day, ground-dropped the apples and had the FFD central office send an email to the customer (Rogers at Frisco) informing them of the same. Sturdevant recalls telling the gatekeeper about the ground drop.

Unfortunately, Conwell was inundated with severe rainstorms, hail, and flash flooding, which destroyed all but 5 percent of the Heritage apples Frisco delivered to Blenheim. Upon discovering the loss on September 29, Pagano tried to contact Rogers and, being unable to do so, reached Rogers's supervisor, Ronnie Gyandoh. Gyandoh took the position that the destroyed apples belonged to Blenheim, while Blenheim (Pagano) relied on the cancellation of the purchase prior to shipment.

Frisco has sued Blenheim for its purchase price for the apples from PRUF of $100,000 plus the shipping cost, $3,000, to get the apples to Blenheim per their order. Blenheim claims it had canceled the order per its contract with Frisco, and the loss is Frisco's.

DEPOSITION OF ADDISON ROGERS

My name is Addison Rogers. I am twenty-nine years old and an actor by profession. When I am between acting jobs, I work a variety part-time jobs to support myself. I live at 4444 Avon Drive in Nita City, Nita. I moved here in YR-5 after receiving my Master of Fine Arts from Nita University School of the Performing Arts. I also have a bachelor's degree in performing arts from Nita State University. I grew up and attended public schools with my two older brothers in Ardmore, Nita, a suburb of Nita City. My brothers were both star athletes in Ardmore and later at the University of Nita. My only significant extracurricular activities involved drama club, and I was in the cast of both the class play and school musical all three years at Ardmore High.

From February to late September of YR-2, I worked as a seller for Frisco Farm Corp., an agricultural broker in Nita City. Frisco was in the business of buying agricultural products from the producers (farms, co-ops, etc.) and selling them mostly to bulk users (supermarket chains, schools, prisons, companies with food service businesses, etc.). There were fifteen or so part-time sellers for Frisco. I worked in Frisco's main office, which was located in Nita City. My manager was Ronnie Gyandoh.

Frisco was a good place to work. We were all friendly and, so long as you did your job, you were allowed to pursue other interests. For me, that was going to auditions for theatrical roles. Everyone at work knew I was an aspiring actor, and people seemed genuinely interested in seeing me succeed. As far as I know, no one complained about my job performance while I was employed at Frisco.

As I said, I was in the sales department. The purchasing department identified products for Frisco to purchase for sale to its customers. Madrid Pinto managed the purchasing department, and they had somewhere between ten and fifteen buyers. The purchasing people and salespeople worked together to determine the price we paid growers and the price we charged customers. Georgie Veramos was one of the people in purchasing with whom I worked on a fairly regular basis. I frequently worked outside of traditional business hours (to accommodate daytime auditions), often staying until 10:00 p.m., when I would do research and catch up on paperwork.

When one of Madrid's buyers identified a producer with goods for sale, they notified one of us in the sales department. They let us know the probable price Frisco would have to pay for the product and when the product would be available for pickup. The buyer and I would figure out the price we would have to charge to our customers to hit Frisco's target profit margin. After that, I would look for potential customers at that price or better. If I found a purchaser at an acceptable price, Frisco would do a virtually simultaneous transaction wherein Frisco bought from a producer and, within a matter of days, sold and delivered the product to that purchaser. To maintain control, Frisco usually shipped through one of its agent shipping companies.

In most cases when purchasing informed us of some product that could be obtained for sale, we already had a buyer in mind, or at least a ready list of entities that typically purchased such items. In some cases, however, we had no regular buyer, or none was interested, so we had to search for one. In those circumstances, we were always on the lookout for a sale to a purchaser typically serviced by another broker, or for a new, potentially long-term customer for Frisco. If we identified a new customer for products, we were eligible for a bonus payment. Frisco paid these awards, if any, on a quarterly basis. I received a bonus during my time at Frisco—in June of YR-2 at the end of the second quarter.

On September 20, YR-2, I was still employed at Frisco. I received a group text from Georgie Veramos. Ronnie Gyandoh and Madrid Pinto—Georgie's supervisor—were also in the text group (Exhibit 1). Georgie said a supplier, Pomes R Us Farms (PRUF), had 25,000 pounds of Heritage apples available for purchase. PRUF is a Nita state-certified organic grower. Organically grown Heritage apples are the most expensive apples available in the market and considered a delicacy. Because of their price, these apples typically are sold only in high-end markets like the Whole Foods stores and, in Nita, the Blenheim Markets stores. PRUF had contacted Georgie with an offer to sell the apples within a seven- to ten-day window when the apples would be picked and available for delivery for a minimum price of $4.00 per pound. Later that same day, and before I began my search for an appropriate buyer, Madrid Pinto responded to the text (Exhibit 1). Madrid had heard that Blenheim Markets was a potential purchaser for the apple crop. I had not considered Blenheim because they worked almost exclusively with HK Brokers for years. But Madrid said there were credible rumors that Blenheim had recently purchased produce from other brokers. Blenheim, as I said, was an upscale chain and a perfect match for the high-end, organic Heritage apples. So, I set about trying to make a deal with them.

I did some quick, informal research and learned that Madrid's information was accurate; other brokers had heard rumors that Blenheim had fallen out with their regular supplier. I identified Sam Pagano as a purchasing agent at Blenheim Markets. I sent Pagano an email inquiring about Blenheim's interest in a 25,000 pound shipment of organic Heritage apples within the next seven to ten days (Exhibit 2). Pagano emailed back that Blenheim was interested in the apples and proposed a price of $4.62 per pound (Exhibit 2). I was really happy with that because it was slightly above our internal target price.

Yes, if Blenheim became a repeat customer for Frisco, I would have been eligible for a bonus. No, I was not aware of any other buyer looking for the Heritage apples. Given Blenheim's immediate interest, and Ronnie Gyandoh's interest in developing a relationship with Blenheim Markets, which is a major produce vendor in Nita, I didn't really work too hard to locate another.

Once I got Pagano's email, I called Georgie Veramos on the phone on September 22 and asked for a firm price of $4.00 per pound for the 25,000 pounds of apples from PRUF. Georgie called back the same day and said that the $4.00 price was good for PRUF, and the apples would be available for delivery within six to nine days.

On Monday September 24, I emailed Pagano at Blenheim Markets proposing the sale of 25,000 pounds of apples at $4.62 per pound with delivery by Frisco with six days. (Exhibit 2). Yes, my email signature shows a business address for Frisco, my name, and two email addresses—one for Frisco generally and one for me at Frisco.

I received a reply email from Pagano that indicated Blenheim Markets was interested and proposed a price. The email also asked for confirmation. I called Pagano shortly after receiving that email, and we verbally agreed to the proposed purchase price of $4.62 a pound, unless Blenheim cancelled the agreement within three business days. When I questioned that proviso, Pagano assured me that the likelihood of cancellation was slim, but Blenheim included it on the chance that something unexpected happened. I accepted this explanation of the cancellation clause without probing for more specific information, and yes, I did so even though I knew about the rumor that Blenheim was available as a customer for Frisco because of a falling out Blenheim had with its regular supplier. I then sent Pagano an email confirming our agreement and the terms of the proposed contract (Exhibit 3).

Honestly, I never put two and two together and, to this day, although I know Blenheim eventually wanted to cancel our deal, I don't know why. At any rate, Frisco purchased the 25,000 pounds of Heritage apples from PRUF at $4.00, with Frisco picking up the apples from PRUF no later than September 29, YR-2 (Exhibit 4).

During our call, Pagano asked whether we utilized an in-house shipping operation. I said our shipping was done through independent contractors, and Pagano suggested that we use Farm Fresh Delivery (FFD), a regular delivery firm for Blenheim, as they had specialized self-unloading equipment they would use for this delivery, and they were familiar with the Blenheim facility, which was quite large and could be confusing in navigating. I knew FFD was probably a little more expensive than Frisco's usual trucking service, but this was a good contract for us, so I used FFD for the delivery. After speaking with a representative at FFD, I sent an email with an attached work order hiring them for the delivery (Exhibits 5 and 6) providing for FFD to pick up the apples on September 29 at PRUF and deliver them to Blenheim Farms, Grocers Way, Yard A unless cancelled on or before September 27. Their price was $3,000.

As it turned out, September 25, YR-2, was my last day at Frisco. I was up for a part in a Netflix series, which required me to be out of town from the last week of September possibly through the first week of October, for auditions, so I had to resign. I notified Ronnie Gyandoh verbally of the fact of my resignation about two weeks before my last day, September 25. I understand that Ronnie now claims no recollection of my quitting, but everyone at Frisco knew I was excited about the part. When I told Ronnie I was leaving I remember asking if, should Blenheim became a repeat customer of Frisco, I would still be considered for a bonus, and they said they would raise it with the boss.

I did receive a letter formally discharging me as an employee for "excessive absenteeism," (Exhibit 7) but not until I returned to Nita City after my audition when I collected my held mail at the post office. I took it at the time as an effort to cheat me out of any Blenheim bonus. Because I did not get the Netflix series, I had to apply for new part-time jobs, and Frisco's claim of "excessive absenteeism" has hurt me unfairly in finding such positions.

No, I did not ask HR at Frisco to shut down my Frisco email address, nor did I notify Blenheim that I was leaving Frisco. No one told me to do so, and Frisco was well aware of the agreement to purchase the apples from PRUF and sell them to Blenheim. Similarly, Blenheim knew that their contract was with Frisco, not me. After all, Ronnie Gyandoh and I had talked about the deal several times, and they were well aware of the particulars. In addition, business emails are copied to both Gyandoh and Madrid Pinto. I don't know why the September 24 series of emails between myself and Blenheim would not have been copied to Gyandoh.

I really don't know what the quarrel is. Blenheim agreed to buy the apples with delivery by the trucking company they suggested unless they cancelled within three business days. Three business days from September 24 is September 27, and Pagano, as I understand it, did not cancel until the fourth business day, September 28.

Fortunately, I have gotten a job with a community theater group in West Haven, Nita. Its rehearsals and meetings are in the evenings, so I am available to go out on auditions. The pay is low, but as part of the job I get a rent-free efficiency apartment located at the West Haven Community Playhouse.

Assuming I don't have an acting job that takes me out of state, I am willing to testify to what I know about this problem.

Signed this 7th day of January, YR-0, at Nita City, Nita.

Addison Rogers
ADDISON ROGERS, deponent Certified by:

ROGER DAVIS
Certified Court Reporter

Deposition of Ronnie Gyandoh

My name is Ronnie Gyandoh. I am thirty-eight years old and have been married to Alex for ten years. Alex and I live with our two children, Hayden, age seven, and Robin, age five, in a small house we just bought at 1805 Charter Drive in Nita City. I grew up in New York City and met Alex while we were both students at the University of Nita. I graduated with a BS in business. Upon graduation, I worked for Nita Whole Foods for ten years. Then I was approached by one of our suppliers, Frisco Farm Corp., and hired as the supervisor for sales in Frisco's tri-state business. I operate out of our regional office in Nita City. Alex, who has a BA degree in psychology with a minor in business, works in the HR department for Minicom, Inc., an electronics company here in Nita City. Our children attend Nita public schools.

Frisco is an agricultural broker. Our business consists of locating agricultural products for sale by producers, buying those products, and then reselling them—mainly to bulk customers like grocery chains and large institutions such as the Nita State Corrections Department. Organizationally, there are two functional departments within Frisco: purchasing and sales. The purchasing department identifies agricultural products from producers such as farms and co-ops, most of which are regular providers. The sales department identifies potential purchasers for those products. Again, most of these purchasers will be regular customers, although Frisco is always looking to increase its client base. Once a match is made, purchasing acquires the agricultural product and almost simultaneously my department, sales, arranges a sale to a grocery chain or other bulk customer. Frisco's delivery agents pick up the products and deliver them to the customer. The gross profit is the difference between the purchase price and the sales price, less the shipping costs. Our headquarters are located in Nita City, and we have satellite offices carrying on the purchase and sales functions throughout the tri-state area. For example, we have a fairly large office devoted to purchasing in western Nita, which is predominantly farming country for both produce and meat chickens.

As I said, my office is in Nita City. Given that our business is dependent on weather and the time when the product is best for delivery to the customer, we regularly conduct business on Saturdays. Several clerical people work for me in the sales department, plus I have approximately fifteen part-time (fifteen to twenty-five hours per week) salespeople. Yes, it is true that part-time workers are cheaper for the company because no benefits are required, but in addition there are many people in the arts, start-up companies, or parents who are looking for extra income. We do pay $18.00 per hour and bonuses on their anniversary date for people who work for at least twelve months. We are also flexible on work hours so long as people get their jobs done.

Yes, I would say that I am a hands-on manager, in part necessitated by our part-time work force. Once the people in purchasing (managed by Madrid Pinto) identify agricultural products that will be coming on the market, they communicate the same to my shop, sometimes directly to one of my employees, but always with copies to myself and Madrid. My people then look for a buyer, work with purchasing to get buy/sell numbers that work for us, and make the deal. In our business, the broker must actually purchase the products from the agricultural producer, given the risk of spoilage, before their product will be released but, in essence, the buy transaction is made simultaneous with the sale transaction, and delivery is made directly from the seller to the buyer. Although we momentarily own the product, we do not have warehousing capability or delivery vehicles.

Yes, I am fully aware of the transaction involving the Heritage apples from Pomes R Us Farms (PRUF) that we sold to Blenheim Markets. I was involved in early decisions to try to attract the Blenheim business (Exhibit 1), I had conversations about it with Addison Rogers (our part-time employee), and have read the documents made available to me (Exhibits 1–5). Exhibit 6 is our work order to FFD for the shipment from PRUF to Blenheim. As far as I am concerned, our agreement was to acquire 25,000 pounds of Heritage apples and deliver them to Blenheim by September 29, YR-2. We did so. I know that Sam Pagano and Blenheim claim they cancelled that transaction, but the plain terms were they had to do so by September 27, YR-2, which they did not do.

Pagano did try to cancel the transaction on September 28, YR-2 and, even though we did not deliver until September 29, the cancellation was outside the date provided in our agreement. Further, the cancellation was not sent to the main Frisco email address, but rather to our former employee, Addison Rogers, at a Frisco email address like the ones we provide all employees. Addison had been let go by the time that email was sent. Finally, Pagano claims that because the final emails making the deal were not delivered until after normal working hours, the three-day cancellation period did not begin until September 25. That is not consistent with any use of the term business day that I have ever encountered.

No, Addison Rogers did not resign from Frisco. We had to let Addison go because of excessive absenteeism (Exhibit 7). We gave two weeks' notice of the termination by mail on September 12, YR-2. We were aware of Addison's acting aspirations and did our best to accommodate auditions, but they became a distraction. The auditions were generally in the daytime, and we are a daytime business. Despite being in the office after hours, Addison was not getting the work done we needed. Now that you mention it, Addison did say something about being up for a role in a Netflix series around the time of the discharge, but that really had nothing whatsoever to do with our termination.

Blenheim claims 95 percent of the shipment of apples was ruined by flooding rains because the apples, rather than being delivered to the conveyor at the Blenheim facility, were unloaded to the ground by Frisco's trucking agent. First, it was not the delivery company's job to make sure the Blenheim apples were preserved. Second, the delivery was made, as agreed to, to Yard A at the Blenheim facility. Third, the delivery was made with the knowledge of Blenheim's gatekeeper, who could have controlled where the apples were unloaded. Finally, although we admit that the shipper, FFD was Frisco's agent, Frisco hired FFD at Sam Pagano's suggestion because Blenheim liked FFD's equipment and its familiarity with Blenheim's facility. FFD was a little more expensive than the trucking service we usually use, but we were getting a good price for the product and we wanted to get Blenheim's repeat business if at all possible.

Signed this 7th day of January, YR-0, at Nita City, Nita.

Ronnie Gyandoh
RONNIE GYANDOH, deponent Certified by:

Roger Davis
ROGER DAVIS
Certified Court Reporter

Deposition of Sam Pagano

My name is Sam Pagano. I am thirty years old, married to my spouse of seven years, Brook, and we live in Nita City in a home left to me by my grandparents, located along Nita Lake at 97 Lakeside Drive. We are renovating that house and plan to be done within a year or two, at which point we hope to start a family. I graduated from Nita State University, where I majored in the food science industry. I chose that major because my grandparents owned an Italian deli (Pagano's on Main Street in Nita City). Even when I was in high school, I dreamed of joining the business. As it turned out, my grandparents decided to sell the business and retire—they gave me their Lakeside Drive house because I was the only grandchild to express any interest in the deli and its business. My grandfather helped me get my current job at Blenheim's; he introduced me to Saul Blenheim, the president of Blenheim Markets (a regional food market chain), who is the son of my grandfather's contemporary, Marv Blenheim, the founder.

At Blenheim's, I acquire produce and other farm goods for sale in our stores. It is very unusual for us to deal directly with the producers of the goods (farms, co-ops, etc.). We normally deal with agricultural brokers. Agricultural brokers are middlemen. They neither grow the product nor sell it to end users, like individual consumers. They just facilitate part of the chain from the growers to the retail consumers, like the shoppers in our markets.

Our purchasing process typically starts with Blenheim's letting an agricultural broker know that we need a particular product. The broker finds a grower with product available, or soon becoming available, and determines the schedule on which the grower can deliver. We come to an agreement with the broker on the price for the goods, and for delivery by a date certain. The broker hires a shipper and gives the shipper the name of the producer, the place of pick-up and our place of delivery, which for Nita County is our yard on Grocers Way in Conwell, Nita.

Over time, Blenheim has built up a number of regular suppliers for certain products. Only for unusual products do we go out onto the open market. From time to time, however, our regular relationship with a broker for a certain kind of product will wane, and we will seek another regular broker for those products.

In September of YR-2, we were in the market for Heritage apples, which are hard to come by and are considered a delicacy among apples. We like to acquire organic product when we can because the customers at our markets prefer that and organic brings us a higher profit margin. Heritage apples are a high-end apple—very crunchy and flavorful—and organic Heritage apples are probably the highest priced apples sold anywhere. We stock them to cater to our customers willing to spend a lot of money for the highest quality products.

Our normal broker for apples was HK Agricultural Brokerage. Unfortunately, Saul Blenheim and Howard Klein, who was the owner and operator of HK, had a personal falling out—no,

I don't know what it was about. All I know is that, on September 7, YR-2, I was directed not to do any business with HK for the foreseeable future. When we were about to go looking for Heritage apples, I checked with Saul's personal assistant, Cheryl Sabine, who confirmed the bad feelings continued. I told her that we needed apples for fall sales. She told me to go ahead and make a deal with another supplier, but wait until necessary to make the deal and build in a three-day escape period, in case the two principals could bring themselves to mend their disagreement.

By September 20, I couldn't wait any longer to stock our retail stores. I put out the word that I was in the market for Heritage apples.

On September 20 I received an email from Addison Rogers at Frisco Farms Corp. inquiring about our interest in purchasing 25,000 pounds of organic Heritage apples (Exhibit 2). I assumed Frisco had somehow caught wind that we were looking for a new supplier, but it just could have been a cold email.

I checked with Ms. Sabine, who gave me the go ahead, and on September 22 I replied to Rogers at the Frisco email address (Exhibit 2) about my interest in the purchase of the apples and proposed a price of $4.62 per pound. I also phoned Rogers and said we were interested and that I needed a few days.

On September 24 Rogers (again on a personal Frisco email) proposed to sell 25,000 pounds of organic Heritage apples at my proposed price of $4.62 per pound, delivery within ten days. I phoned Rogers, said we were interested, and suggested Frisco consider using our regular shipper, Farm Fresh Delivery (FFD), because they had the equipment we liked for gentle treatment of the product and efficient offloading at our facility. I said I would respond as soon as I could.

On September 24, YR-2, which was a Monday, after one last check with Ms. Sabine on whether to go through on the purchase, I got the go-ahead. It was after hours but I wanted to get the order out. I sent an email to Rogers (at the same Frisco email address) at 7:00 p.m., offering to purchase 25,000 pounds of organic Heritage apples at $4.62 per pound, delivery within six days, unless cancelled within three business days.

On September 24 at 8:00 p.m., I got a reply email from Rogers agreeing to my previous email. By that time I had gone home and did not see the email until the next day.

On September 28 Cheryl Sabine called and told me that Saul and Howard had made up and to cancel the apple order. I immediately sent an email to Rogers at Frisco cancelling the deal (Exhibit 3).

On September 30 I got a panicked phone call from Jayden Lewis, the manager of our Grocers Way facility in Conwell, Nita. Jayden told me that what looked like over 20,000 pounds of apples had been ground-dropped at Yard A the day before and that, due to the torrential rains and hail in Conwell, all but a small portion was ruined. I asked who had made the delivery, and Jayden said FFD. I asked Jayden to check my list of orders, which is sent to the gatehouse each day, to see if the delivery was scheduled. It was not. I then spoke to the gatekeeper, Flynn Stowe, who told me Riley Sturdevant delivered the apples. Riley's father owns FFD, so Flynn knows Riley well. Even though the delivery wasn't on the gate list, Riley had a work order for the delivery of the apples from PRUF to Blenheim, with the broker listed as Frisco, so Flynn allowed the truck in to make the delivery.

I immediately called Addison Rogers at Frisco. That extension was routed to supervisor Ronnie Gyandoh, who said that Addison had left the company for another opportunity. I pointed out my cancellation of the deal and Gyandoh responded that the cancellation had to have been made within three days of the September 24 agreement. I told Gyandoh that I had provided for a three-business-day cancellation and that, although my cancellation was on September 28, our deal was completed after the close of business on September 24, so that three business days would have been September 28, which was when I cancelled.

Gyandoh also said that my email was sent to Addison and that this deal was with Frisco so that if I wanted to cancel, I should have sent it to the Frisco business email. Gyandoh said that even though the cancellation was after the three day window, if Frisco had received notice before the shipment actually occurred (on September 29) something might have been worked out, but under the circumstances, the contract stands.

I followed up with Riley Sturdevant of FFD, and who apologized about the error, but said that FFD just followed the contract that had been made with Frisco, and that the gatekeeper had not stopped the truck. Riley admitted that it was very unusual not to be met at Yard A with an unloading crew to move the produce to the storage building, but that it really did not raise any red flags at the time because of FFD's very tight schedule for that day.

Signed this 9th day of January, YR-0, at Nita City, Nita.

Sam Pagano
SAM PAGANO, deponent Certified by:

ROGER DAVIS
Certified Court Reporter

Deposition of Riley Sturdevant

My name is Riley Sturdevant. I am twenty-seven years old, single, and I work as a driver for Farm Fresh Delivery (FFD), which is owned by my father, Dan Sturdevant. My siblings have no interest in the business, so my dad has frequently said that I will inherit the business when he retires. I live in a one-bedroom condo Dad purchased for me. It is true that I went through a wild period when I was younger and have two arrests and convictions for possession of marijuana, both misdemeanors, while I was in high school. I also have a felony arrest for joy-riding when I was nineteen for which I pled guilty to a misdemeanor. I served sixty days in the county jail and two years' parole.

When I got out of jail, I went to work for my father, working around the shop doing custodial and maintenance work. By the time I was twenty-two and off parole, I was able to get my CDL license to drive trucks and started driving for FFD.

FFD is a farm products delivery company. We are hired by farms, agricultural brokers, wholesalers, and market chains to transport fresh produce. We own two specialized belt trailers for handling agricultural products. To prepare an order, we take a trailer to the farm's lot and the farmer loads it. Then I return with the truck cab that pulls the trailer, hook up, and go make the delivery. Our belt trailers are what they call "walking floor" trailers; they have a specialized, self-unloading belt. When I get to the delivery point, where the receiving company usually has a conveyor and operators, I hook the chute on the back of the trailer to the front of the conveyor and start up the trailer's belt. The trailer does the rest and brings out the whole load onto the customer's conveyor.

Our customers include several large supermarket companies, whose produce we transport from their central warehouse yard to their various retail outlets. In addition, we do a lot of work for agricultural product brokers who buy produce from farms and co-ops and then sell almost immediately to a customer like a grocery chain, a school, or an institution. When we work for the brokers, we are their agents, and yes, we take our direction from them. Our regular work week includes Saturdays and, in emergencies, Sundays.

One of our best customers is Blenheim Markets. Their main produce storage facility is on Grocers Way in Conwell, Nita. It is a ten-acre facility with fifteen loading yards for dropping off purchased products and picking up products for deliveries to their retail stores.

On September 24 we got a call from an Addison Rogers at Frisco Farm Corp., who said Blenheim Markets had referred us and Frisco wanted to contract with us for pick-up of 25,000 pounds of Heritage apples from Pomes R Us Farms (PRUF) on September 29 for delivery to Blenheim Markets, Grocers Way, Yard A, Conwell, Nita. Exhibit 4 is the email Rogers sent from Frisco that had the work order attached. Exhibit 5 is the work order for that job. I also know that we billed them, and they made a direct deposit payment for the job (Exhibit 6).

Not having heard anything to the contrary, we picked up the apples from PRUF and delivered them to Blenheim on September 29, which was a Saturday. Blenheim's facility is open seven days a week, with full crews every day except Sunday. I was the driver on the delivery. The pick-up was without complication. I did run into some difficulty when I reached Blenheim, where I had made literally a hundred deliveries. I reached the Blenheim gate and told the gatekeeper I had a load of apples for Yard A. The gatekeeper told me Blenheim's list of scheduled deliveries did not include this delivery. I looked at my work order, which showed Addison Rogers as the person at Frisco who made the order. I tried to call Frisco, but could not reach Rogers. That is when I noticed that the work order did not list a responsible Blenheim person for me to contact, either.

At any rate, I was running late on another job. The gatekeeper recognized me, reviewed my work order, and let me in. I went, as the papers directed, to Yard A. When I got there, there was no crew to offload the apples. The yard was empty and there was literally no one around, it being lunch time. I probably should have waited for someone to show up, but because I was in a hurry, I just ground-dropped the apples in Yard A, figuring the crew would get to them with their equipment after lunch.

As I left the facility, I paused at the gate and the gatekeeper asked how it went. I responded, "all offloaded at Yard A." I did not mention that the delivery was to the ground, not to an off-loading crew. I guess I felt a little guilty, and of course I didn't know that Sam Pagano from Blenheim had canceled order. None of this would have happened if the Rogers person had listed Pagano as the Blenheim ordering representative. In that case, I wouldn't have ground-dropped the apples without Pagano's go-ahead. As I said, Blenheim was one of our major clients.

Signed this 9th day of January, YR-0, at Nita City, Nita.

Riley Sturdevant
RILEY STURDEVANT, deponent Certified by:

Roger Davis

ROGER DAVIS
Certified Court Reporter

EXHIBITS

Exhibit 1A

Texts Between Veramos, Rogers, Pinto, and Gyandoh

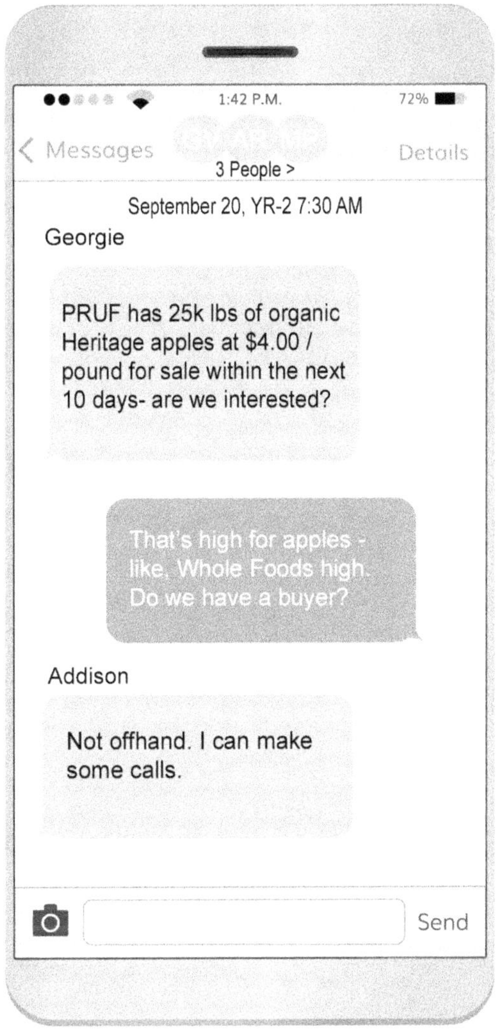

Exhibit 1B

Texts Between Veramos, Rogers, Pinto, and Gyandoh (cont.)

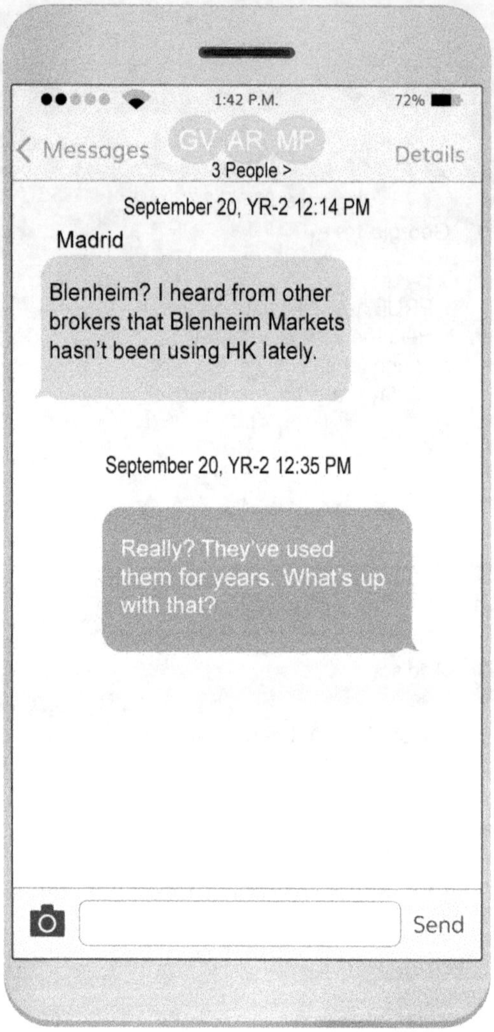

Exhibit 1C

Texts Between Veramos, Rogers, Pinto, and Gyandoh (cont.)

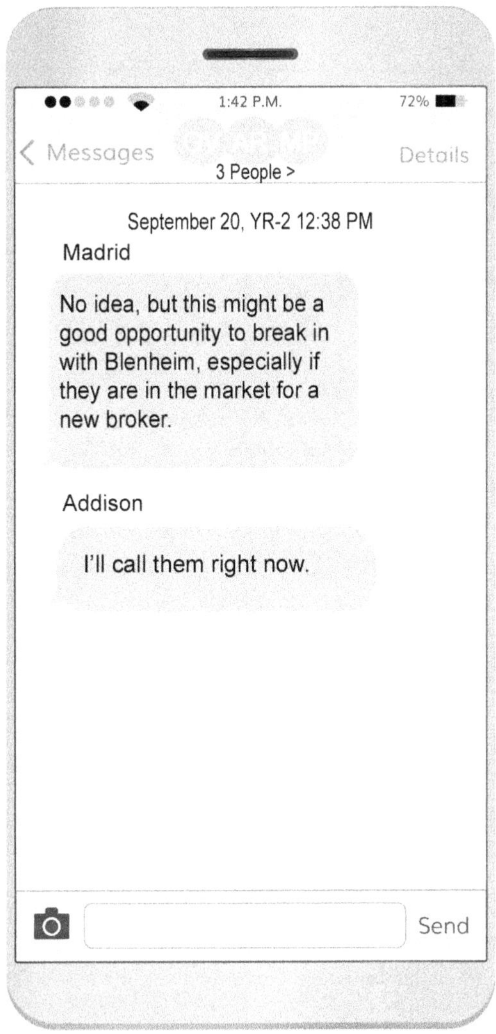

Exhibit 2

Addison Rogers

From:	Sam Pagano <sam.pagano@blenheimmarket.nita>
Sent:	Sep 21, YR-2 11:33 AM
To:	Addison Rogers <arogers@friscofarm.nita>
Subject:	re: Heritage Apples

Addison,

We are interested. Our proposed price is $4.62 per pound for the Heritages—get back to me.

Sam

From:	Addison Rogers <arogers@friscofarm.nita>
Sent:	Sep 20, YR-2 9:28 AM
To:	Sam Pagano <sam.pagano@blenheimmarket.nita>, <main@friscofarm.nita>
Subject:	Heritage Apples

Dear Sir:

We have available for sale within the next nine days 25,000 lbs of organic Heritage apples. Any interest?

Addison Rogers

Frisco Farm Corp.
37592 Calliope Lane
Nita Valley, Nita
819-555-3827
info@friscofarm.nita

Exhibit 3

Addison Rogers

From: Sam Pagano <sam.pagano@blenheimmarket.nita>
Sent: Sep 28, YR-2 1:06 PM
To: Addison Rogers <arogers@friscofarm.nita>
Subject: re: Heritage Apples Order

Addison,

Unfortunately, we have to cancel our agreement for the purchase of 25,000 lbs. of Heritage apples at $4.62 per lb. I hope we can do business in the future.

Sam

From: Addison Rogers <arogers@friscofarm.nita>
Sent: Sep 24, YR-2 8:13 PM
To: Sam Pagano <sam.pagano@blenheimmarket.nita>
Subject: re: Heritage Apples Order

Sam,

We have a deal on the terms stated in your communication of today. Hope we can begin a long relationship with Blenheim.

Addison

From: Sam Pagano <sam.pagano@blenheimmarket.nita>
Sent: Sep 24, YR-2 7:04 PM
To: Addison Rogers <arogers@friscofarm.nita>
Subject: Heritage Apples Order

Addison,

Consistent with our phone conversation today, we propose a sale by Frisco to Blenheim of 25,000 pounds of organic Heritage apples at $4.62 per lb. Delivery within 6 days, unless agreement cancelled within 3 business days from the contract date.

Sam

Exhibit 4

Addison Rogers

From:	Addison Rogers <arogers@friscofarm.nita>
Sent:	Sep 24, YR-2 3:37 PM
To:	Farm Fresh Delivery <orders@farmfreshdelivers.nita>
CC:	Ronnie Gyandoh <rgyandoh@friscofarm.nita>
Subject:	Heritage Apples Order
Attachment:	Work Order

Please find attached your work order form.

Addison Rogers

Frisco Farm Corp.

37592 Calliope Lane
Nita Valley, Nita 57829
819-555-3827
info@friscofarm.nita

Exhibit 5

Farm Fresh Delivery

Work order

Order placed by: Frisco Farm Corp., Account #FF3w366

Order #13554 (September 24, YR-2)

Service	Date	Pickup Location	Delivery Location	Price
Transport 25,000 lbs apples	09/29/YR-2	Pomes R Us Farms	Blenheim Markets	$3000

Contact: Addison Rogers arogers@friscofarm.nita 819-555-3827

Delivery Contact:

Special Instructions: Pick up/deliver 09/29/YR-2 unless cancelled on or before 09/27/YR-2

Subtotal:	$3000.00
Payment terms:	EFT 2 business days after delivery
Total:	$3000.00

FS

Exhibit 6

Ronnie Gyandoh

From:	Ronnie Gyandoh <rgyandoh@friscofarm.nita>
Sent:	Sep 30, YR-2 7:49 AM
To:	Farm Fresh Delivery <orders@farmfreshdelivers.nita>
Subject:	re: Heritage Apples Order—Work Order

Confirming EFT deposit to bank account provided by FFD $3,000 payment in full for delivery 09/29/YR-2 of 25,000 lbs apples from PRUF to Blenheim Markets.

Ronnie

Frisco Farm Corp.

37592 Calliope Lane
Nita Valley, Nita 57829
819-555-3827
info@friscofarm.nita

From:	Farm Fresh Delivery <orders@farmfreshdelivers.nita>
Sent:	Sep 28, YR-2 4:34 PM
To:	Frisco Farms <info@friscofarm.nita>
Subject:	re: Heritage Apples Order—Work Order

Apples dropped at Blenheim yard A 4pm today. Riley

Exhibit 7

POMES R US FARMS

97771 State Route 12
Apple Valley, Nita

Old-Time Apples for That Old-Time Delicious Flavor

INVOICE

Date: 9/29/YR-2, pay on pickup

BILLING ADDRESS
Frisco Farm Corp.
37592 Calliope Lane
Nita Valley, Nita

SHIPPING ADDRESS

Shipping by buyer

QTY	ITEM	DESCRIPTION	PRICE
25,000 LBS	HERITAGE	PICKED & LOADED	$4.00 LB

PAID

Total	$100,000.00
Shipping	0.00
Tax	0.00
Amt. due	$100,000.00

THANK YOU VERY MUCH FOR YOUR BUSINESS

Disclaimer: Purchase price as shown on the face of this invoice. No credits, refunds or exchanges. All sales are final.

Exhibit 8

Frisco Farm Corp.

37592 Calliope Lane
Nita Valley, Nita 57829

819-555-3827
info@friscofarm.nita

September 12, YR-2

Ms. Addison Rogers
PO Box 73
Nita City, NI

Dear Addison:

It is with some regret that Frisco Farm must provide you with two weeks' notice and terminate your employment as a sales representative, effective September 26, YR-2.

As you know, your acting career goals, which require many auditions during regular business hours, while initially acceptable, have become a problem with excessive daytime working absenteeism becoming the norm.

Thank you for your employment with Frisco and best of luck in your future endeavors.

Sincerely,

Ronnie Gyandoh

Ronnie Gyandoh

Exhibit 9

ARREST AND CONVICTION RECORD

Defendant Information

Number:	130752
Name:	RILEY STURDEVANT
Status:	CLOSED
Date of Birth:	1/17/YR-27

Charges

Type	Date	Charge Description	Disposition
INDICT	6/25/YR-11	MIS DRUG POSSESSION	NOLLE $100 FINE
INDICT	8/14/YR-11	MIS DRUG POSSESSION	NOLLE $250 FINE
INDICT	6/22/YR-8	FEL LARCENY	PLD GLTY- N/C - IND @ P/T

Felony Case Actions

Event Date	Event Description
09/23/YR-6	PROBATION COMPLETE
09/23/YR-8	LEAVING JAIL
07/24/YR-8	ENTER JAIL
07/22/YR-8	SENTENCED
07/22/YR-8	PLEA
07/22/YR-8	ARRAIGNED
06/25/YR-8	INDICTED BINDOVER
06/23/YR-8	BAIL
06/22/YR-8	JAIL
06/22/YR-8	TRANSCRIPT FILED
06/22/YR-8	BINDOVER CIF#CI064083Y
06/22/YR-8	ARRESTED

Exhibit 10

SEPTEMBER, YR-2

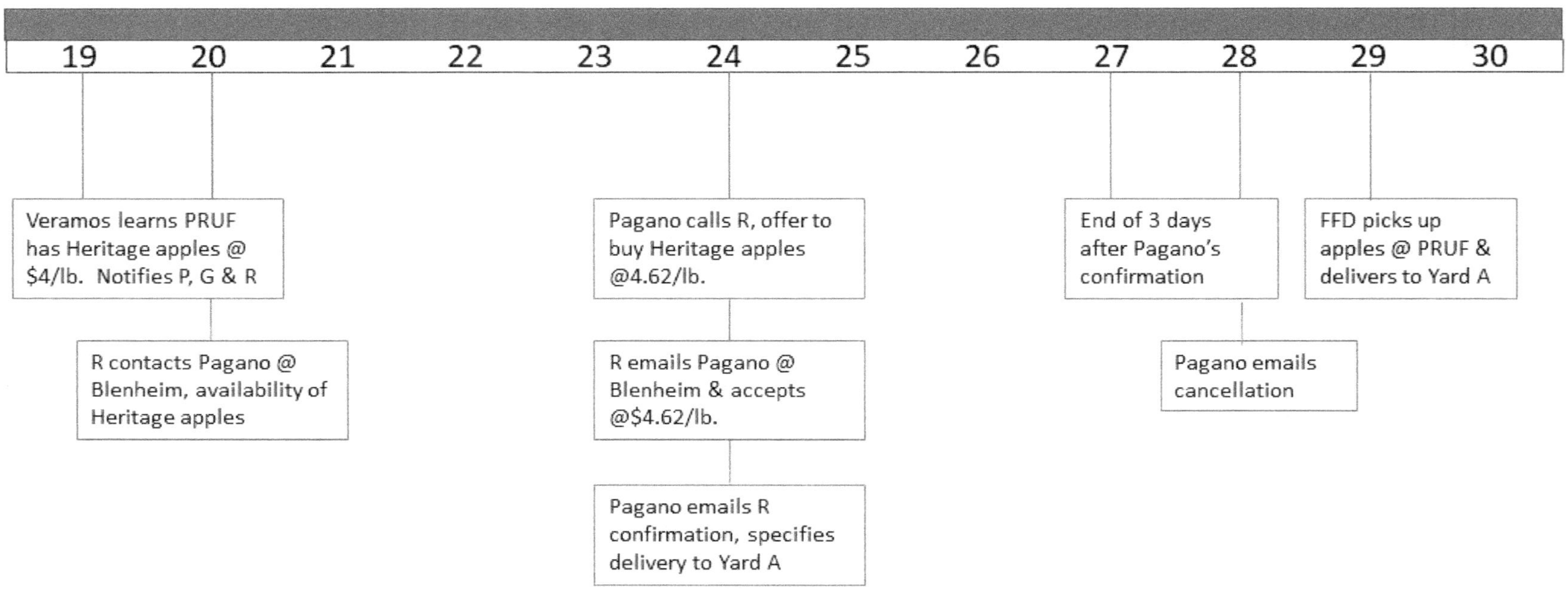

General Jury Instructions

1. Nita Instruction 01:01—Introduction

You have been selected as jurors and have taken an oath to well and truly try this cause. This trial will last one day.

During the progress of the trial, there will be periods of time when the Court recesses. During those periods of time, you must not talk about this case among yourselves or with anyone else.

During the trial, do not talk to any of the parties, their lawyers, or any of the witnesses.

If any attempt is made by anyone to talk to you concerning the matters here under consideration, you should immediately report that fact to the Court.

You should keep an open mind. You should not form or express an opinion during the trial and should reach no conclusion in this case until you have heard all of the evidence, the arguments of counsel, and the final instructions as to the law that will be given to you by the Court.

2. Nita Instruction 01:02—Conduct of the Trial

First, the attorneys will have an opportunity to make opening statements. These statements are not evidence and should be considered only as a preview of what the attorneys expect the evidence will be.

Following the opening statements, witnesses will be called to testify. They will be placed under oath and questioned by the attorneys. Documents and other tangible exhibits may also be received as evidence. If an exhibit is given to you to examine, you should examine it carefully, individually, and without any comment.

It is counsel's right and duty to object when testimony or other evidence is being offered that he or she believes is not admissible.

When the Court sustains an objection to a question, the jurors must disregard the question and the answer, if one has been given, and draw no inference from the question or answer or speculate as to what the witness would have said if permitted to answer. Jurors must also disregard evidence stricken from the record.

When the Court sustains an objection to any evidence the jurors must disregard that evidence.

When the Court overrules an objection to any evidence, the jurors must not give that evidence any more weight than if the objection had not been made.

When the evidence is completed, the attorneys will make closing arguments. These arguments are not evidence, but are given to help you evaluate the evidence. The attorneys are also permitted to argue in an attempt to persuade you to a particular verdict. You may accept or reject those arguments as you see fit.

Finally, just before you retire to consider your verdict, I will give you further instructions on the law that applies to this case.

3. Nita Instruction 2:01—Introduction

Members of the jury, the evidence and arguments in this case have been completed, and I will now instruct you as to the law.

The law applicable to this case is stated in these instructions, and it is your duty to follow all of them.

You must not single out certain instructions and disregard others.

It is your duty to determine the facts and to determine them only from the evidence in this case. You are to apply the law to the facts and in this way decide the case. You must not be governed or influenced by sympathy or prejudice for or against any party in this case. Your verdict must be based on evidence and not on speculation, guess, or conjecture.

The evidence that you should consider consists only of witness testimony and exhibits the Court has received.

Any evidence that was received for a limited purpose should not be considered by you for any other purpose.

You should consider all the evidence in the light of your own observations and experiences in life.

4. Nita Instruction 2:02—Opening Statements and Closing Arguments

Opening statements are made by the attorneys to acquaint you with the facts they expect to prove. Closing arguments are made by the attorneys to discuss the facts and circumstances in the case and should be confined to the evidence and to reasonable inferences to be drawn therefrom. Neither opening statements nor closing arguments are evidence, and any statement or argument made by the attorneys that is not based on the evidence should be disregarded.

5. Nita Instruction 2:03—Credibility of Witnesses

You are the sole judges of the credibility of the witnesses and of the weight to be given to the testimony of each witness. In determining what credit is to be given any witness, you may take into account his ability and opportunity to observe; his manner and appearance while testifying; any interest, bias, or prejudice he may have; the reasonableness of his testimony considered in the light of all the evidence; and any other factors that bear on the believability and weight of the witness's testimony.

6. Nita Instruction 2:04—Burden of Proof

When I say that a party has the burden of proof on any issue or use the expression "if you find," "if you decide," or "by a preponderance of the evidence," I mean that you must be persuaded from a consideration of all the evidence in the case that the issue in question is more probably true than not true.

Any findings of fact you make must be based on probabilities, not possibilities. It may not be based on surmise, speculation, or conjecture.

Jury Instructions Specific to this Case

The Court now will instruct you as to the claims and defenses of each party and the law governing the case. You must arrive at your verdict by applying the law, as I now instruct you, to the facts as you find them to be.

1. Background—Basic Contentions of the Parties

The parties to this case are Frisco Farm Corporation (hereinafter Frisco), the plaintiff, and Blenheim Markets (hereinafter Blenheim), the defendant. Frisco has sued Blenheim seeking to recover damages based on a claim that Blenheim failed to pay for certain goods as required by a contract. Both sides agree to the following:

1. That Blenheim offered to purchase 25,000 tons of Heritage Apples from Frisco at a price of $4.62 per pound to be delivered by Frisco to Blenheim by Oct 3, YR-2.
2. That the contract was created by an offer to buy the apples by Blenheim at the sales prices contained in an email from Sam Pagano, an agent of Blenheim, to Addison Rogers, an agent of Frisco, on September 24, YR-2, at 7:04 p.m.
3. That Frisco accepted the offer by Blenheim in an email from Rogers to Pagano dated September 24, YR-2 at 8:13 p.m.
4. That the Blenheim offer allowed it to cancel the order within three business days of the formation of the contract.
5. That on September 28 at 1:06 p.m., Pagano sent an email to Rogers at Frisco that purported to cancel the agreement between the parties to purchase apples.
6. That on September 29, YR-2, Fresh Farm Delivery, an agent of Frisco, delivered 25,000 pounds of Heritage apples to Blenheim at Grocers Way in Conwell, Nita.

2. Damages—General

If Frisco prevails, its damages will be predicated on the price of the goods that it shipped to Blenheim, agreed to be 25,000 at $4.62 per pound pus shipping costs of $3,000. If Blenheim prevails, its damages are nothing.

3. Existence of a Contract

You first must decide whether Frisco has proven that there was a contract for the sale of the apples to Blenheim. Frisco has the burden of proving this issue by the preponderance of the evidence. Frisco must prove all elements of the contract about which the parties do not agree. Frisco must prove that there was an offer, an acceptance, and mutual assent.

An offer is an expression of one's willingness to be bound by a contract.

An acceptance is an expression of assent to the offer.

Mutual assent occurs when an offer is communicated by one party to another and is accepted by the other party. Whether there was mutual assent must be determined from the conduct of the parties.

Whether the conduct of the parties constituted an offer and acceptance and, if it did, what its meaning was depends on what reasonable persons in the positions of the parties would have thought they meant. In determining what reasonable persons would have thought the conduct meant, you should consider the evidence as to all circumstances existing at the time of the offer or acceptance. You should not consider any different, but unexpressed meanings intended by either party.

Frisco must also prove that the goods were delivered to Blenheim. You must consider all facts and circumstances in deciding whether Frisco made the delivery.

4. What Constitutes a Business Day in the State of NITA?

The parties agree that there was an agreement between the parties to purchase 25,000 pounds of Heritage Apples at $4.62 per pound and that delivery was to be made to Blenheim. At its essence, the question for you to decide is whether three days from the creation of the contract had passed between September 24, YR-2 at 8:13 p.m. and September 28, YR-2 at 1:06 p.m. If you decide that three business days had passed before the purported cancellation of the contract by Blenheim on September 28, YR-2, at 1:06 p.m., then I instruct you to find for the plaintiff.

5. Parol Evidence

The court has determined that in making your decision you may consider parol evidence, which means that in deciding on the meaning of the written contract document, you may consider the previous oral declarations of the parties that are not stated in the contract document itself.

The parties agree on the following facts:

a. At all times relevant Addison Rogers was an agent of Frisco.
b. At all times relevant Sam Pagano was an agent of Blenheim.
c. At all times relevant Farm Fresh Delivery and Sturdivant were agents of Frisco for the purposes of delivery of the apples in question.
d. At all times relevant Flynn Stowe was an agent of Blenheim for the purposes of performing his employment as gatekeeper of Blenheim's storage facility.

IN THE SUPERIOR COURT
IN AND FOR THE COUNTY OF DARROW
AND STATE OF NITA

FRISCO FARM CORPORATION	)	
	)	
Plaintiff,	)	CIVIL ACTION
	)	YR-1:2342
v.	)	
	)	
BLENHEIM MARKETS	)	SPECIAL VERDICT FORM #1
	)	**[LIABILITY ONLY]**
Defendant.	)	

PART I

1. Did Frisco prove unanimously, and by a preponderance of the evidence, that a contract existed between Frisco and Blenheim for the sale of 25,000 pounds of Heritage Apples, that Frisco delivered the goods to Blenheim, and that Blenheim failed to pay for the goods? Yes _____ No _____.

If your answer is no, your deliberations are over. Enter a verdict for BLENHEIM, the defendant.

If you answer is yes, continue to Part II.

PART II

2. Did Blenheim prove unanimously, and by a preponderance of the evidence, that the contract provided that Blenheim could cancel the contract for the purpose 25,000 tons of Heritage Apples within three business days of the making of the contract between Frisco and Blenheim on September 24, YR-2, at 8:13 p.m., and that Blenheim's purported cancellation of September 28, YR-2, at 1:06 p.m. was within three business days?

   Yes ____ No ____

If your answer is yes, your deliberations are over. Enter a verdict for BLENHEIM, the defendant.

If your answer is no, enter a verdict in favor of FRISCO in the amount of $118,500.

VERDICT

For the Plaintiff in the amount of $ _________________.

For the Defendant: _____________________.

If the verdict is unanimous, the Foreperson should sign the verdict.

IN THIS VERDICT EACH OF US CONCURS.

Foreperson _______________ Date _________________

IN THE SUPERIOR COURT
IN AND FOR THE COUNTY OF DARROW
AND STATE OF NITA

FRISCO FARM PRODUCTS	)	
	)	
	)	
Plaintiff,	)	CIVIL ACTION
	)	YR-1:2342
v.	)	
	)	
BLENHEIM MARKETS	)	SPECIAL VERDICT FORM #2
	)	**[DAMAGES ONLY]**
Defendant.	)	

We, the jury, and each of us finds:

For the plaintiff in the amount of $ __________.

For the Defendant ________________.

[You may answer either question 1 or question 2, but not both.]

Foreperson _______________ Date __________________

www.ingramcontent.com/pod-product-compliance
Lightning Source LLC
LaVergne TN
LVHW080000210926
848481LV00012B/3633
* 9 7 8 1 6 0 1 5 6 9 3 8 7 *